S0-BED-972

The Nightingale

as retold by Midori Seto
illustrated by Stacey Schuett

SCHOOL PUBLISHERS

Copyright © by Harcourt, Inc.

All rights reserved. No part of this publication may be reproduced or transmitted in any form or by any means, electronic or mechanical, including photocopy, recording, or any information storage and retrieval system, without permission in writing from the publisher.

Requests for permission to make copies of any part of the work should be addressed to School Permissions and Copyrights, Harcourt, Inc., 6277 Sea Harbor Drive, Orlando, Florida 32887-6777. Fax: 407-345-2418.

HARCOURT and the Harcourt Logo are trademarks of Harcourt, Inc., registered in the United States of America and/or other jurisdictions.

Printed in China

ISBN 10: 0-15-350530-3
ISBN 13: 978-0-15-350530-0

Ordering Options
ISBN 10: 0-15-350334-3 (Grade 4 Below-Level Collection)
ISBN 13: 978-0-15-350334-4 (Grade 4 Below-Level Collection)
ISBN 10: 0-15-357522-0 (package of 5)
ISBN 13: 978-0-15-357522-8 (package of 5)

If you have received these materials as examination copies free of charge, Harcourt School Publishers retains title to the materials and they may not be resold. Resale of examination copies is strictly prohibited and is illegal.

Possession of this publication in print format does not entitle users to convert this publication, or any portion of it, into electronic format.

5 6 7 8 9 10   985   12 11 10 09

A very long time ago in China, an emperor lived in a beautiful palace. Around the palace was a garden. Many of the flowers and trees in the garden had bells tied to them. When the wind blew the bells jingled.

Beyond the garden was a forest. In this forest lived a nightingale. Its song was so sweet that when people heard it, they would stop what they were doing. When people walked through the forest, they agreed the nightingale had the most beautiful song of all the birds.

One day, the emperor overheard his servants talking about the little bird and resolved to find out more. The emperor longed to hear this bird's song. He said to one of his servants, "You must find this bird and bring her to me."

The servant looked through the garden, but she could not find the bird. Then the servant went into the forest. She asked a fisher about the nightingale. "Oh, yes," said the fisher, "I have heard the song of this bird."

"Please take me to her," said the servant.

The fisher led the servant through the forest. As they walked along, a cow started to moo. "Oh my, what a very powerful voice for such a little bird," exclaimed the servant.

"Oh, no," said the fisher, "that is only the mooing of a cow."

Then they heard the croaking of some frogs. "Oh, what a lovely song," said the servant. "This bird has the sound of tinkling little bells."

"No," sighed the fisher, "those are only frogs."

Suddenly, the fisher stopped and pointed to a little bird that sat upon a branch. The bird was not stingy with her song and sang happily for the servant and the fisher.

"Such a beautiful song coming from such a plain little bird," said the servant.

Then the servant said to the bird, "Little nightingale, the emperor wishes that you would sing for him at the palace."

"My song sounds best in the forest," replied the nightingale sadly, "but if the emperor says I must come then I suppose I have no choice."

That night, the noble emperor sat on his throne. Next to his throne stood a golden perch for the bird. Many people had gathered to hear the nightingale.

All eyes were on the nightingale as she began to sing. Her song was so lovely and forlorn that tears came to the emperor's eyes. The beautiful song of this bird touched all the people at the court.

The emperor was so pleased that he commanded the little bird to stay at his palace. She was given a golden cage and twelve servants. All through the city, people talked about the wonderful little bird.

One day, the emperor received as a gift a toy nightingale that looked like a real bird but was covered in lovely jewels. When the toy bird was wound up, it sang just like a real nightingale. All who saw the toy bird thought it was very beautiful and that its song was lovely, too.

"Now the two birds must sing together," declared the emperor. The birds sang, but they did not sound good together. The toy bird sang the same song over and over again. The real nightingale sang in her own beautiful way.

Surprisingly, all the people at the palace
thought the toy bird's song was as lovely as the
nightingale's. They thought the toy bird prettier,
too, with all its wonderful jewels.

The real nightingale was terribly unhappy.
She wanted to be free to live in the forest that she
loved. One day, someone forgot to close the door
of the nightingale's cage. She quickly escaped
and flew away to her real home in the forest.

"I did so much for that ungrateful bird," cried
the emperor angrily. "I will never let her in the
palace again." All the people in the palace agreed
with the emperor.

Meanwhile, the people wanted to listen to the toy bird. It didn't matter that it sang the same song over and over again. The emperor placed the toy bird in the gold cage, and every night the toy bird would sing for the emperor and the people in the palace.

Back in the forest the real bird sang. The fisher listened to its lovely song. He considered it rather pathetic that the people of the palace preferred the toy bird.

A year passed, and every night the emperor and the people of the palace would gather around the toy bird and listen to it sing. They knew every note of the song, and it still did not matter that the bird could only sing one song.

Then one night, a suspicious whirring sound came from the toy bird. Suddenly, a spring broke inside the toy bird. The bird's song began to slow down, and then the bird fidgeted and stopped singing. "The bird is broken! What shall we do?" moaned the emperor, and he called the royal watchmaker.

The royal watchmaker scrounged for parts to repair the toy bird. Finally, the watchmaker gave up and reported back to the emperor. "I am afraid I cannot repair the bird. She is worn out." This news caused great sorrow for the people of the palace and the emperor.

Five years passed. Then one day, the emperor became very ill. The royal doctor told the people of the palace, "I am afraid the emperor will not live much longer. He is much too ill." This made the people of the palace very sad for they were very fond of their leader.

Back in the forest, the real nightingale heard of the emperor's illness. She flew to the palace and sat at his window. Then the little bird began to sing her sweet song.

As he listened to the bird's lovely song, the emperor began to feel better. "Please sing again," said the emperor. The nightingale sang for the emperor all that night.

The emperor begged the little bird to stay with him forever. "I cannot leave my real home in the forest again," said the nightingale, "but I will come and sing for you every night."

This made the emperor feel very joyful. "You have saved my life, little bird," he said. "I will never tell anyone our secret."

With that, the nightingale flew away. In the morning, the emperor awoke feeling strong and well. The people of the palace entered his bedroom, fearing the worst. Before them sat the emperor who smiled and said, "Good morning!"

Think Critically

1. Tell in order the events that led up to the nightingale singing for the emperor the first time.

2. How does the emperor feel when he hears the real nightingale for the first time?

3. What did the nightingale do when someone left the door of her cage open?

4. What do you think is special about the real nightingale's song?

5. Would you change the ending of this story? How?

 Math

Make a Graph Ask your classmates whether they would rather hear the real nightingale or the toy one. Keep a tally of their answers. Then make a graph to show your findings.

 School-Home Connection Share this story with a family member. Retell the story in your own words.

Word Count: 1,089